I'll join in and observe the kitchen staff and pupils.

I'll interview the school cook, the head teacher and the local authority school meals' superviser.

I'll design a simple questionnaire for 7 to 11 year old pupils.

I'll try and get some parents to take part in a discussion on school meals.

CHOOSING A TOPIC

There are many reasons for choosing a particular research topic. Here are a few.

VALUES

Ann Oakley, a feminist, wanted to bring women's issues centre stage. Her male colleagues in the 1960s were puzzled that she chose to study something as 'insignificant' as housework.

MORALITY

Peter Townsend (1928-2009) was driven by his convictions. He spent over 50 years researching poverty and campaigning on behalf of the poor.

ISSUES

Choosing a research topic is influenced by the issues of the day, for example, globalisation.

FUNDING

The choice of topic may be influenced by the priorities of the funding organisations.

Soci...tures

Rese... ...lition

Michael ...

with Wendy ...

...Matt Timson

Contents

Published by Collins Educational and Odeon Books

An imprint of HarperCollins Publishers, 1 London Bridge Street, London SE1 9GF

© Michael Haralambos, 2016
First edition 2012, second edition 2016
ISBN 978-0-00-819669-1

Michael Haralambos asserts his moral rights to be identified as the author of this work.

British Library Cataloguing in Publication Data.
A catalogue record for this publication is available from the British Library.

Typography and design by John A Collins

Printed and bound in the UK by Bishops

Thanks To Peter Langley who, with Michael Haralambos, developed the idea of sociology in pictures. And thanks to Catherine Steers and Kimberley Atkins at Collins Educational for their support.

Note In many cases, the speech bubbles are

Dedication To Charlie, Sammy, Lucy, Max, ... Woody

Starting research involves thinking of a topic to study and deciding what methods to use to collect the information.

Sociologists choose a research topic that interests them and that they think is important.

Researchers often begin in the library, reading studies on their chosen topic.

Research in schools serving Jamie Oliver's 'healthy meals' showed improvements in Key Stage 2 test results and a 15% drop in absences due to illness (Belot and James, 2009).

The British Sociological Association's ethical guidelines state that people should be made aware that they are participating in research.

PARTICIPANT OBSERVATION

Participant observation is a research method which involves the researcher taking part in the activities of those they are studying.

HANGING OUT

Sudhir Venkatesh studied the Black Kings, an African-American gang who sold crack in Chicago. He began with a questionnaire survey which he quickly replaced with participant observation (Venkatesh, 2009).

Questionnaire

How does it feel to be black and poor?

- ☐ Very bad
- ☐ Somewhat bad
- ☐ Neither bad nor good
- ☐ Somewhat good
- ☐ Very good

Part of Sudhir's questionnaire.

RIGHT, QUESTION 1. HOW DOES IT FEEL TO BE BLACK AND POOR?

Sudhir reads from his questionnaire.

YOU AIN'T GOING TO LEARN NOTHING WITH THIS! WITH PEOPLE LIKE US YOU SHOULD HANG OUT AND GET TO KNOW WHAT WE DO.

JT the gang leader gives Sudhir some advice.

LOOK, LISTEN AND STAY IN THE BACKGROUND.

'I took JT's advice and hung out with the gang. They didn't like interview questions. They probably had enough of that from cops and social workers. So I just made small talk. In general, I said very little.'

GAINING ENTRY

One of the difficulties of participant observation is gaining entry into the group. It helps if important members are on your side.

DAY 1

DAY 2

DAY 3

ACTING NORMALLY

Researchers want to observe people behaving normally. They do their best not to influence those they observe. This can be seen from research by David Hargreaves (1967), who studied teachers and students in a boys' secondary school in northern England. For part of his research, he sat at the back of the classroom and observed what was going on.

DAY 1

DAY 5

TURN AROUND AND PAY ATTENTION, BOYS.

'At first my presence caused changes in the boys' behaviour. But once the boys got used to me, they behaved normally.'

THE TEACHERS PUT ON A SHOW FOR YOU – SMILES AND ALL THAT.

IF YOU WEREN'T THERE, MR O WOULD GET REAL MAD.

WHEN YOU'RE IN HE TRIED TO ACT CALMLY AS THOUGH HE'S A LITTLE ANGEL.

'Many of the teachers appeared to behave quite naturally and act as if I was not in the room at all. But it is difficult to check on the extent of the changes my presence produced.'

STREET CORNER SOCIETY

In 1937, William Foote Whyte began a 3½ year study of an Italian-American gang in Boston. Based on participant observation, this classic study was called *Street Corner Society*.

'As I sat and listened, I learned the answers to questions I would not have had the sense to ask if I had been getting my information solely on an interviewing basis' (Whyte, 1943).

'The gambler's jaw dropped. He glared at me. For the rest of that evening I felt very uncomfortable.'

Next day, Doc the gang leader, said, 'Go easy on that who, what, why, when stuff Bill. You ask those questions and people will clam up on you.'

Doc worked closely with Bill. 'Now, when I do something, I have to think what Bill Whyte would want to know about it and how I can explain it. Before, I used to do things by instinct.'

OBSERVATIONS IN CONTEXT

Participant observers look at what people do in their normal, everyday settings, how they make sense of their experiences and how they act in different situations.

FIDDLING

Jason Ditton (1977) worked for over a year in a bakery in order to observe the fiddles that took place and how the workers saw them.

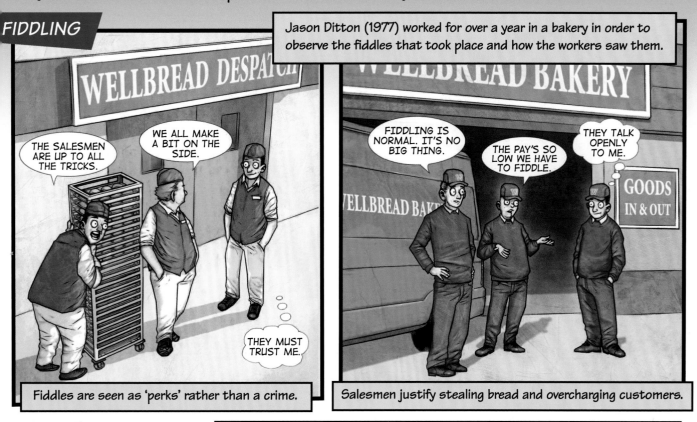

Fiddles are seen as 'perks' rather than a crime.

Salesmen justify stealing bread and overcharging customers.

MANLY FLAWS

Elliot Liebow (1967) spent 1½ years observing African-American men in Washington D.C. The men were either on welfare or in low-paid jobs. Their income was insufficient to support a wife and family. Most had failed marriages.

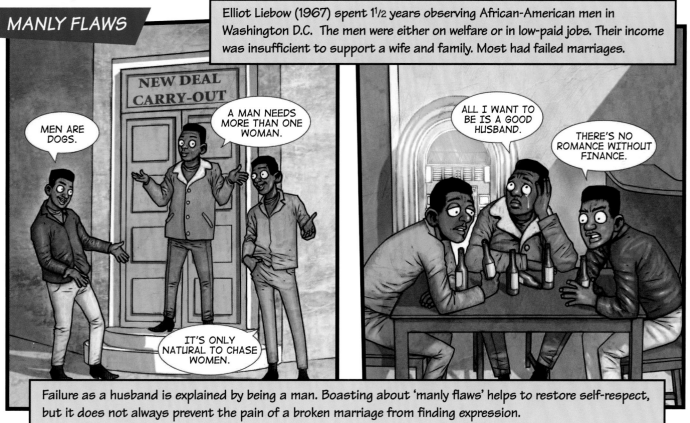

Failure as a husband is explained by being a man. Boasting about 'manly flaws' helps to restore self-respect, but it does not always prevent the pain of a broken marriage from finding expression.

ETHNOGRAPHY

Ethnography is the study of the way of life of a group of people. It aims to see their world from their perspective. Ethnographers argue that the best way to do this is to immerse yourself in their everyday life using participant observation as the main research method.

Bronislaw Malinowski (1884-1942) was one of the founding fathers of ethnography. He spent two years living with the Trobriand Islanders in the Western Pacific.

I'M HERE TO STUDY YOUR WAY OF LIFE.

THE GARDEN MAGICIAN WILL GIVE ME A GOOD CROP

The aim of ethnography is to 'grasp the native's point of view... to realise his vision of his world' (Malinowski, 1922).

Trobriand men spend half their lives gardening. The garden magician conducts ceremonies to help the crops grow.

THAT'S A FINE YAM HARVEST.

WELL DONE.

I FEEL REALLY PROUD. PEOPLE WILL LOOK UP TO ME.

MY JOB IS TO SEE GARDENING THROUGH THEIR EYES.

At harvest time men display their crops. People walk from garden to garden admiring the best crops and praising the best gardeners.

PARTICIPATING ONLINE

Virtual worlds are online worlds such as *Second Life, World of Warcraft, Dreamscape* and *EverQuest*. Participant observation is a valuable research method for studying these worlds.

PREPARATION

To participate in virtual worlds, the researcher must learn the rules, roles and conventions of the game. For example, in her study of *World of Warcraft*, Bonnie Nardi had to learn the roles of a raider and a night elf priest (Boellstorff et al, 2012).

COMMUNICATION ONLINE

Tom: My avatar hasn't got any wings!

Party Host: I'll send you some wings.

Participant observation of virtual worlds often involves online communication with other players. This can be seen from Tom Boellstorff's study of *Second Life* when he was invited to a 'wings dance party' (Boellstorff, 2006).

COMMUNICATION OFFLINE

Sometimes game players meet in the physical world. T.L.Taylor met 30 people who played the game she was studying. This led to a discussion of her avatar (her online virtual person) who had a female head and a male body. The discussion covered the main themes of her research – embodiment, identity and performance (Taylor, 2002; Boellstorff et al, 2012).

INVOLVEMENT

Celia Pearce (2006, 2009) studied an online game called *Buggy Polo*. She tried not to influence the players and stayed on the sidelines. They told her she was too detached. She got more involved and in doing so gained the trust and respect of the other players.

NON-PARTICIPANT OBSERVATION

In non-participant observation the researcher does not participate directly with those they are observing and is therefore less likely to influence their behaviour. However, compared to participant observation the researcher has fewer chances to discover the meanings which direct the behaviour of those they observe.

OBSERVING CARS

This study was designed to test the view that wealthy, upper-class people were more uncaring and selfish than those lower down the social scale. The study assumed that cars indicated wealth and position in society.

SELFISH..!

IT'S NOT HIS TURN!

SHE SHOULD HAVE STOPPED!

Observers found that the more expensive and newer the car, the more likely drivers were to cut off other vehicles rather than wait their turn at 4-way intersections. And the less likely they were to stop for people at pedestrian crossings (Piff et al, 2012).

STRUCTURED OBSERVATIONS

Structured observations use an *observation schedule* which tells the researcher how, when and what to look for and how to categorise and record their observations.

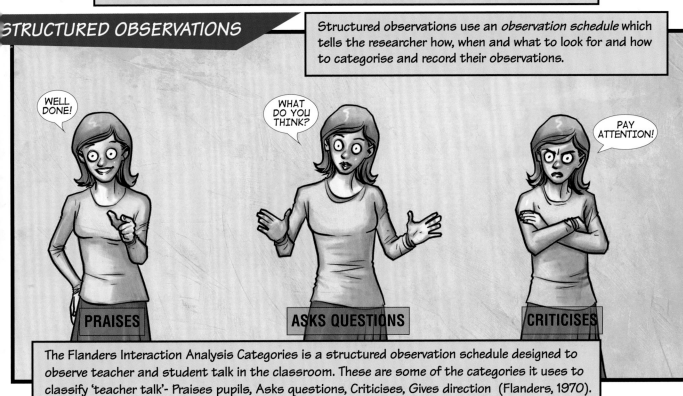

WELL DONE!

WHAT DO YOU THINK?

PAY ATTENTION!

PRAISES

ASKS QUESTIONS

CRITICISES

The Flanders Interaction Analysis Categories is a structured observation schedule designed to observe teacher and student talk in the classroom. These are some of the categories it uses to classify 'teacher talk'- Praises pupils, Asks questions, Criticises, Gives direction (Flanders, 1970).

TYPES OF INTERVIEW

STRUCTURED INTERVIEW

This is a structured interview — it is a questionnaire read out to the interviewee.

UNSTRUCTURED INTERVIEW

This is an unstructured interview — it is less directed and more like a conversation.

RAPPORT

Interviewers are often advised to establish rapport — a warm and friendly relationship with the interviewee.

ASSERTIVENESS

Howard Becker (1971) sometimes used a more assertive approach which may lead people to be 'considerably more frank than they had originally intended'.

FEMINIST INTERVIEWING

Some feminists argue that interviews should be woman to woman. The interviewer should express sympathy and understanding based on shared experience and treat the interviewee as an equal.

INTERVIEW EFFECTS

Interviews can be influenced by the age, gender, status, ethnicity and social class of the interviewer and the interviewee, by the way they see each other and by the setting in which the interview takes place.

DEFINING THE INTERVIEWER

In a study of organisational culture, Martin Parker (2000) found that interviewees defined him in different ways. These definitions influenced the answers they gave.

SOCIAL DESIRABILITY EFFECTS

People tend to present themselves in the best possible light in interviews. This can lead to an emphasis on socially desirable aspects of their behaviour.

GOING TO CHURCH

A survey conducted by Gallup found that 35% of Episcopalians in the USA said that they had been to church in the last 7 days. Yet figures from the churches showed that only 16% actually did so (Bruce, 1995).

TAKING COCAINE

Over 600 Chicago residents were asked if they had taken cocaine in the last year. After the interview, 571 agreed to take a drugs test. Around three-quarters of those testing positive for cocaine use did *not* report taking it (Johnson et al, 2002).

INTERVIEWS IN CONTEXT

The following interviews were used to assess the linguistic skills of African-American boys (Labov, 1973). The boys were asked to describe a toy plane.

INTERVIEW 1

The boy sees the interview as threatening. He gives short answers followed by long silences.

INTERVIEW 2

This time the interviewer is black but the boy's responses are similar to those in Interview 1.

INTERVIEW 3

The interviewer and the boy are the same as in Interview 2. The setting is more informal, the boy's best friend is present and they are supplied with crisps. The boy is now confident, talkative and gives a detailed description of the plane.

FOCUS GROUPS

Focus groups are a way of collecting data from several people. They are sometimes called *group interviews*. However, they are often more like discussions. Group members are encouraged to talk amongst themselves. They are guided by a *moderator* or *facilitator* who asks them to focus on particular topics.

BODY IMAGE

Five focus groups each made up of 4 boys or men of similar ages were asked to discuss body image, diet and exercise. They were more likely to disclose sensitive, personal feelings in a small group of people like themselves rather than in a one-to-one interview situation (Grogan and Richards, 2002).

AT EASE

Sarah Grogan, who conducted the body image study with Helen Richards.

MODERATING

The moderator should encourage everyone to contribute and prevent some from discouraging others. In each of the above cases the moderator might: 1) avoid eye contact and turn away, 2) emphasise that everyone's opinion is valuable, 3) directly ask for their views, 4) gently ask for their opinion, nod and make eye contact (Kruger and Casey, 2009; Braun and Clarke, 2013).

People sometimes say different things in different groups. For example, boys and men tend to be more 'macho' and boastful in all-male focus groups than in male and female groups or in a one-to-one situation with a female interviewer (Wight, 1994).

ONLINE FOCUS GROUPS

There are many different types of online focus groups. The following study uses conferencing software. The participants – young mothers and expectant mothers – type their contributions to the discussion and the moderators type their guidance. The topic is parenting (O'Connor and Madge, 2001).

Focus group members sitting at home and typing their contributions to the discussion.

Kerry is a focus group participant, Hen and Clare are moderators. As mothers with young children Hen and Clare found they could relate to the focus group and build rapport.

ONLINE INTERVIEWS

This unit looks at online text-based interviews in which questions and answers are typed. In general, email interviews tend to be longer and the answers more considered than interviews conducted in chat-rooms and social media.

But it is unlikely to provide a cross-section of the population as a whole because low-income groups are less likely to have access to a computer.

For people who are shy and lacking in confidence, facing a screen rather than an interviewer may produce a better interview.

Online interviews usually take longer than face-to-face interviews, especially if the interviewee is not very good at typing.

However, this reduces the possibility of interviewer bias.

No travel, it's all online. No typing the answers, just print them off.

Body language and facial expressions are not available in text-based interviews. And emotions are difficult to convey. Emoticons (short for emotion icon) may help, though they are a poor substitute.

VIRTUAL WORLD INTERVIEWS

Virtual worlds are not simply fantasy and fun. Many participants experience 'rich, meaningful and enduring social interaction with people they never meet offline' (Boellstorff et al, 2010). Interviewing in virtual worlds has many aspects in common with interviewing in the physical world. But there are important differences.

WHO ARE WE INTERVIEWING?

This picture shows a person in the physical world (on the left) and her three avatars who live in a virtual world. An avatar is a virtual person you create.

Avatars can be extensions of the self, an idealised self, a variation of the self or a brand new self. Interviewing both the participant and their avatars can add to an understanding of an online community and the creation of identity, both online and offline.

AT HOME

Interviewed in the comfort and privacy of their virtual home, an avatar will be more likely to speak freely and openly.

SHOPPING

Residents in *Second Life* virtual world can buy a wide range of goods and services with virtual currency. The more we know about this community, the more relevant our interview questions.

QUESTIONNAIRES

CONSTRUCTING A QUESTIONNAIRE

Questionnaires are lists of questions. They should be clear and straightforward and mean the same thing to everybody who answers them. Here are some of the dos and don'ts of questionnaires.

AVOID OVERSIMPLIFICATION

What do you think about abortion?

- [ ] Good
- [ ] Bad
- [ ] No opinion

FAR TOO COMPLICATED TO ANSWER BY TICKING A BOX.

AVOID LEADING QUESTIONS

Any reasonable person is against keeping animals locked up in zoos.

Do you agree?

THEY'RE LEADING ME TO SAY YES.

BE SPECIFIC

Do you drink coffee often?

IS 16 CUPS A DAY OFTEN?

KEEP THE LANGUAGE SIMPLE

McDonald's are ubiquitous.

Do you agree?

????

AVOID EMOTIVE LANGUAGE

Should a racist, sexist, homophobic, vicious, anti-social, right-wing extremist be given a job in a nursery school?

WELL, IF YOU PUT IT LIKE THAT, NO!

KEEP IT SHORT

Question 281

zzzz zzz

ANSWERING QUESTIONS

When answering questions, people sometimes say one thing and do another. And sometimes they say things they believe to be true which are not actually true.

YES AND NO

In the 1930s, a young Chinese couple visited 250 hotels and restaurants in the USA. Only once were they refused service. Letters were sent to the places they visited asking would they accept Chinese guests. 92% said 'no', 7% 'uncertain' and 1% 'yes' (LaPiere, 1934).

FALSE MEMORIES

In a study of memory, 36% of adult Americans recalled a childhood meeting with Bugs Bunny at Disneyland. This could not have happened since Bugs Bunny is not a Disney character (Loftus, 2003).

Children were given a list of horror videos, some with fictitious titles such as *Blood On The Teeth Of The Vampire*. 68% claimed to have seen one or more of the fictitious films (Cumberbatch, 1994).

OPERATIONALISATION

Operationalisation is putting a concept into a form which can be measured. It starts with an *operational definition* which makes an abstract concept into something concrete and measurable. The next step is to break the definition down into *indicators* which can be used to measure it. This unit looks at the operationalisation of religious belief.

PLACES OF WORSHIP

An operational definition of religion might be a belief in some form of supernatural power. Attendance at places where people worship a supernatural power has been used as an indicator of religious belief and as a measure of its extent.

Does church attendance indicate religious belief? In Victorian Britain going to church was often seen as a sign of middle-class respectability. For some people this may have been the main reason for church attendance. (Martin, 1969).

A study in Ohio estimated church attendance from reports by clergy and from counting cars in church car parks. It found attendance was half that claimed by people in surveys. Other studies in the USA have produced similar results (Hadaway et al, 1993).

BELIEF IN GOD

A belief in some form of God is often used as one of the main indicators for measuring religious belief. Much of this data comes from surveys based on questionnaires. The questions below are 'closed questions'. They provide pre-set answers to choose from.

	1991		2008	
I don't believe in God.	10.16%	124	18.03%	356
I don't know if God exists and there is no way to find out.	13.76%	168	18.64%	368
I don't believe in a personal God but I do believe in some kind of higher power	12.69%	155	14.29%	282
I believe in God some of the time but not at others.	12.69%	155	12.92%	255
I have doubts but I feel that I do believe in God.	25.55%	312	18.09%	357
I know God really exists and I have no doubts about it.	23.26%	284	16.82%	332
Don't know	0.16%	2	-	0
Not answered	1.72%	21	1.22%	24
Total		1,221		1,974

God exists. Do you:
- Strongly agree ☐
- Agree ☐
- Don't know ☐
- Disagree ☐
- Strongly disagree ☐

Surveys like this allow researchers to quantify the results – present the results in the form of numbers (National Centre for Social Research, 2010).

This question is designed to measure the strength of religious belief. The answers are easy to quantify.

CODING

Coding is a means of classifying respondents' answers. Sometimes researchers use pre-coded questions in which respondents are asked to choose one of several pre-set answers. Sometimes respondents are asked to give their own answers which are then coded by the researcher using a list of possible answers. Coding makes it possible to quantify answers – put them into numbers.

> I LIKE PRE-CODED QUESTIONS. ALL I HAVE TO DO IS COUNT THE PEOPLE WHO TICKED EACH ALTERNATIVE.

1. 17
2. 12
3. 26
4. 42

The responses to the British Social Attitudes Survey on page 24 are pre-coded into seven possible choices.

> DO YOU BELIEVE IN GOD?

> IT DEPENDS WHAT YOU MEAN BY GOD. IS GOD ALL-POWERFUL? CAN WE CHANGE GOD'S BEHAVIOUR? DOES GOD CONTROL OUR WORLD? I COULD GO ON AND ON!

Answers such as this are difficult if not impossible to code.

RELIABILITY AND VALIDITY

Quantitative methods involving operational definitions and pre-set answers are often seen as more reliable. Qualitative methods which allow people to answer in their own way are often seen as more likely to produce valid data.

> HOW CAN THE RESULTS OF SIMILAR STUDIES BE COMPARED UNLESS THEY ARE OPERATIONALISED IN THE SAME WAY?

1. 17
2. 12
3. 26
4. 42

Data are reliable if different researchers using the same methods, the same definitions and measurements and a similar sample, produce the same results.

> HAVING TO CHOOSE BETWEEN THE PRE-SET ALTERNATIVES OF CLOSED QUESTIONS DOESN'T ALLOW ME TO SAY WHAT I REALLY THINK AND FEEL.

Data are valid if they present a true and accurate picture of what they are intended to measure.

SAMPLING METHODS

A social survey involves the collection of the same type of data from a fairly large number of people. Social surveys are usually based on samples drawn from the group to be studied – for example, a sample of young people or a sample of women. The data usually come from questionnaires or from structured interviews.

REPRESENTATIVE SAMPLES

Ideally samples should be representative – they should reflect the group as a whole. If the sample is representative, then the findings of the survey are more likely to apply to the wider society.

SIMPLE RANDOM SAMPLES

The researcher obtains a list of names, such as a register of college students. Every name is given a number and the sample is selected by using a list of random numbers. Simple random samples are not necessarily representative.

STRATIFIED RANDOM SAMPLES

A stratified random sample reflects the population as a whole in terms of different groups or strata, such as age or ethnic groups. The sample is randomly selected from one or more of these groups.

A quota sample is like a stratified random sample but the selection is not random. The researcher just fills their quota – e.g., 20 men and 20 women – with the first available people.

SNOWBALL SAMPLES

A snowball sample builds up like rolling a snowball. The researcher finds one person to fit the sample, that person finds another and so on. This is useful when people do not want to be identified or are difficult to find – e.g., criminals, drug addicts and sex workers. Snowball sampling is unlikely to produce a representative sample.

VOLUNTEER SAMPLES

UNIVERSITY RESEARCHER

INVITES

WOMEN

TO DISCUSS THEIR

EXPERIENCE OF MARRIAGE

IN A CONFIDENTIAL INTERVIEW

TEL: 01234 56789

Volunteer samples are drawn from people responding to adverts. Those who volunteer may have a particular reason for doing so – they may have a strongly held point of view or a grievance to express. This may result in an unrepresentative sample.

RESPONSE RATES

The response rate is the percentage of the sample that participates in the research. A low response rate can lead to an unrepresentative sample. Those who don't participate may be significantly different from those who do.

Postal questionnaires often have a low response rate. Responders tend to be better educated than non-responders.

Response is more likely if the researcher drops off and picks up the questionnaire and explains the research.

Language difficulties can lead to low response rates.

The subject matter can affect the response rate. In one study, 19% of the sample refused to participate when they found that it was about incest (Russell, 1986).

Many families refused to participate in the Department of Health study of children's weight. Those with overweight children were more likely to refuse (Bryman, 2008).

Only 61% of a sample of 2,000 offenders agreed to take part in a Home Office survey of probation. The non-responders may have had more negative experiences of probation (Mair, 2000).

A longitudinal study looks at the same group of people over a period of time. The National Child Development Study in Britain began with a sample of 17,400 newborn children in 1958. By 2008, the sample, now aged 50, was down to 9,790 due to death, emigration, failure to trace and refusal to participate. This probably resulted in a less representative sample (ESDS, 2011).

ONLINE SURVEYS

Online surveys are questionnaires self-completed online. They are usually considerably cheaper and quicker than offline surveys. Samples are often larger and cover a wider geographical area. This unit looks at the Global Drug Survey, an online survey of drug users. In 2014 it received nearly 80,000 responses from 17 countries. Participants are anonymous and self-selected (*Global Drug Survey: 2014 Findings*, 2014).

TAKING PART

People are much more likely to complete an anonymous online survey than talking to a complete stranger on the phone or in their home about a sensitive issue such as personal drug use.

THE 2012 GLOBAL DRUG SURVEY

DRUG USERS

15,500 worldwide
7,700 from UK
4,000 from USA and Canada
The rest mainly from European and English speaking countries

UK RESPONDENTS

Average age 28
90% white
55% educated to degree level or higher
Just over 2/3 male
Nearly 3/4 in work
Above average income for age group

SURVEY EXCLUDES OR UNDER-REPRESENTS

Excludes some groups with high level drug use, e.g. the homeless, those in prisons. Under-represents low-income and less well educated.

In the UK the survey was promoted online by the Guardian newspaper, and Mixmag which describes itself as 'The World's Biggest Dance Music and Clubbing Magazine'. (Source: Global Drug Survey: Methodology: 2014)

TYPES OF DATA

Data are the information used in research. There are two main types of data – quantitative and qualitative data.

QUANTITATIVE DATA

Quantitative data are data in the form of numbers.

In 1971 in the UK there were 205,000 women in higher education, 33% of all higher education students. In 2014/15 there were 1,273,000 women, 56% of all higher education students (HESA, 2016).

In Britain in 1974, 51% of men smoked cigarettes, in 2014, 20%. For women, 41% smoked in 1974, 17% in 2014 (ASH, 2016).

In England and Wales there were 352,000 marriages in 1981 and 262,000 in 2012 (Office for National Statistics, 2016).

Qualitative data are all types of data that are not in the form of numbers. They include data from observations and interviews, from written sources such as diaries and newspapers, and from pictorial sources such as paintings and posters.

QUALITATIVE DATA

Gathering qualitative data from observations of fans at a football match.

Collecting qualitative data from a discussion after the match.

Taking notes during an in-depth interview with a fan.

QUALITATIVE RESEARCH

In recent years qualitative research methods such as participant observation and in-depth, unstructured interviews have become increasingly popular.

QUALITATIVE RESEARCH METHODS

Virginia Braun and Victoria Clarke, authors of *Successful Qualitative Research* (2013).

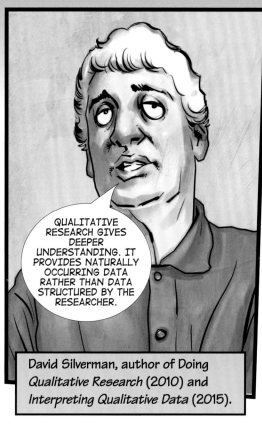

David Silverman, author of *Doing Qualitative Research* (2010) and *Interpreting Qualitative Data* (2015).

MIXED METHODS

A growing number of researchers are seeing a combination of qualitative and quantitative methods as particularly valuable. This is known as *mixed methods research*.

Unstructured interviews can provide in-depth data. They can also provide data to construct relevant and meaningful questions for questionnaires.

MIXED METHODS

A mixed methods approach combines qualitative and quantitative methods, for instance, participant observation and questionnaires. It aims to get the best of both worlds. The example of mixed methods below is taken from *Goth: Identity, Style and Subculture* (2002) by Paul Hodkinson. He had been a Goth for ten years when he conducted the research.

PARTICIPANT OBSERVATION

Participant observation at the Whitby Gothic Weekend. This festival is 'the ultimate experience in taking part in the Goth scene'.

QUESTIONNAIRES

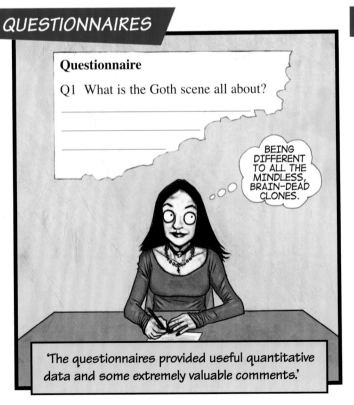

'The questionnaires provided useful quantitative data and some extremely valuable comments.'

INTERVIEWS

The conversation in the interviews was 'open and flowing'. They provided 'in-depth, quality information'.

TRIANGULATION

Like mixed methods, triangulation is a research design which uses a variety of methods. It can also involve a number of different researchers. Triangulation aims to 1) provide a more complete and rounded picture and 2) check on the validity of research findings.

The following example of triangulation was used by Sandra Walklate and her research team in a study of the fear of crime in two high crime urban areas in northern England (Walklate, 2000).

SOCIOLOGY DEPARTMENT

The research team. Being an all-women team may have been an advantage – 'we posed no threat'.

Getting to know the research area with the help of police officers.

Going to pubs and chatting to locals.

CRIME RATE

In-depth interviews with professionals such as social workers and probation officers who work in the area.

Observing police/community meetings.

Analysis of local newspapers.

Mature students from a local university conducting a house-to-house survey.

Focus group discussions with some of the survey participants.

Postal questionnaires sent to local businesses and organisations, followed by telephone interviews with those who agreed to take part.

Talking about triangulation.

RELIABILITY AND VALIDITY

If different researchers using the same methods obtain the same results, then the methods and the results are reliable. But this does not necessarily mean they give a true or valid picture. Nor does it mean that the conclusions drawn from the data are valid.

The observations are reliable – everybody observes the same thing. But the conclusion is not valid – the sun does NOT go round the earth.

Yakima Native American children got low scores on IQ tests because they did not finish in time. Yakima culture placed little importance on speed. The tests were not a valid measure of their intelligence – they mainly reflected the children's culture (Klineberg, 1971).

REDFIELD'S OBSERVATIONS

LEWIS'S OBSERVATIONS

In the late 1920s, Robert Redfield (1930) studied the village of Tepoztlan in Mexico. He found a close-knit, harmonious and happy community. Oscar Lewis (1951) studied the same village 17 years later. He saw the community as divided by envy, distrust and conflict. Redfield and Lewis believed the main reason for these differences resulted from differences between them in terms of their outlook and personality. If so, their observations were not reliable. Nor were they valid – at best they were one-sided.

ASSESSING VALIDITY

We have already looked at various ways of assessing whether research findings are valid – accurate and true. This unit examines some additional methods.

RESPONDENT VALIDATION

This method involves the researcher showing their findings to the research participants and asking them to judge their validity.

Beverly Skeggs (1994) states that this was 'the most common response' to one of her studies.

Michael Bloor (1997) asked doctors to assess his research on their decision-making in medical cases. He queried their replies because, 1) they may not be aware of how and why they made their decisions, 2) they may feel criticised and therefore reject his findings.

RESEARCH COLLABORATOR

Sometimes a research participant works so closely with the researcher that they become a collaborator and help to assess the findings.

'Much of our time was spent in a discussion of ideas and observations so that Doc, the gangleader, became, in a very real sense, a collaborator in the research. He gave me his detailed criticisms' (Whyte, 1993). See page 8.

PREDICTING BEHAVIOUR

Aaron V. Cicourel (1976) observed probation officers in order to discover the meanings they used to define young people as delinquents.

Cicourel found that if a young person was working class, from a low-income, single parent family, and had poor school performance they were likely to be defined as a delinquent. He argued that if he could predict on the basis of these factors who would be defined as delinquent, then this validated his findings.

EXPERIMENTS

LABORATORY EXPERIMENTS

This laboratory experiment tests the statement that noise has an effect on memory.

Participants are asked to recall a list of words. Some are placed in a quiet room, others with loud music. Everything else is the same. If there are differences in recall between the two groups, this suggests that noise affects memory.

Laboratory experiments have been criticised as artificial. If so, they may not reflect behaviour in the 'real' world.

FIELD EXPERIMENTS

Field experiments take place in normal, everyday settings.

This experiment looked at the effect of factors such as lighting on productivity. The results were confusing. For example, productivity increased whether lighting was increased or decreased.

The workers knew they were being observed – this is what affected their productivity. This is known as the Hawthorne effect.

RESEARCH METHODS **39**

CORRELATION

If two things are correlated, then they increase and decrease together, or when one increases, the other decreases. This may be due to one causing the other, to a third factor which causes both, or due to chance.

CHANCE

In Copenhagen for the 12 years following World War Two, the number of storks nesting in the city and the number of human babies born went up and down together. This correlation is probably a coincidence – due to chance.

A THIRD FACTOR

There is a correlation between yellow grass and the sale of cold drinks. The yellower the grass, the more cold drinks are sold. This correlation is probably due to a third factor – the temperature.

TESTING HYPOTHESES

An hypothesis is an expected relationship between two or more factors. It is designed to be tested against evidence. Experiments are often used to test hypotheses. Hypotheses are often drawn from theories.

The self-fulfilling prophecy theory states that someone's expectations of another person will tend to influence that person's behaviour.

Robert Rosenthal and Leonora Jacobson (1968) designed an experiment to test the hypothesis that teachers' expectations of children's ability will affect their progress. They began by giving an IQ test to primary school pupils.

The researchers gave the teachers false information. The names on the list were a random sample of pupils, NOT those with the highest scores.

The pupils were given a second IQ test 8 months after the first. In general, those on the list made greater gains in IQ.

The results of the experiment appeared to support the researchers' hypothesis. Later experiments have produced similar results but others have not.

MULTIPLE CAUSES

Often events are caused by a number of things – they have multiple causes. This can be seen from the dramatic decline of crime in the USA in the 1990s and the early 2000s.

ZERO TOLERANCE POLICING

In 1994, zero tolerance policing began in New York – the police clamped down on all crimes, however small. Within 2 years, murder was halved and robberies were down by a third (Chaundary and Walker, 1996).

VARIOUS FACTORS

The US economy grew and unemployment fell between 1992 and the mid-2000s. The age group with the highest crime risk (15-29) dropped from 27.4% of the population in 1980 to 20.9% in 2000. Police numbers increased by 14% in the 1990s (Zimring, 2007).

PRISON

The US prison population grew from 500,000 in 1980 to 2.4 million in 2011.

GUN CONTROL

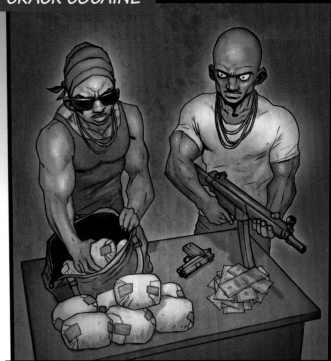

There were sharp falls in handgun homicides in cities like Washington D.C. with strict gun control laws. But there were also sharp falls in cities like Houston where it was easy to buy guns (McGreal, 2011).

CRACK COCAINE

The crack epidemic saw a rise in violent crime as rival gangs fought to control the trade and addicts robbed to feed their habit. The demand for crack declined from the mid-1990s as did violent crime (McGreal, 2011).

TARGET HARDENING

Target hardening – for example, surveillance and electronic security – has made it increasingly difficult to break into buildings and vehicles (McGreal, 2011).

CASE STUDIES

A case study is a detailed study of one particular case or instance of something – for example, a study of an individual, group or community.

LIFE HISTORIES

A life history is a case study of a particular individual – their life as they see it – taken from a series of in-depth interviews.

Mike Maguire (2000) obtained the life history of a 'specialist country house burglar'. The life history method allowed him to 'probe much more deeply than one-off interviews'.

Margot Liberty obtained the life history of John Stands In Timber, one of the last Cheyenne to recall their traditional way of life. 'His kind of inside view will never be achieved again' (Stands In Timber and Liberty, 1967).

A COMMUNITY

Paul Heelas and Linda Woodhead (2005) used Kendal, a town of around 28,000 in the Lake District, for a detailed case study of spirituality and religion. They found a rise in spirituality and a decline in religion. However it is not possible to make generalisations from a single case study.

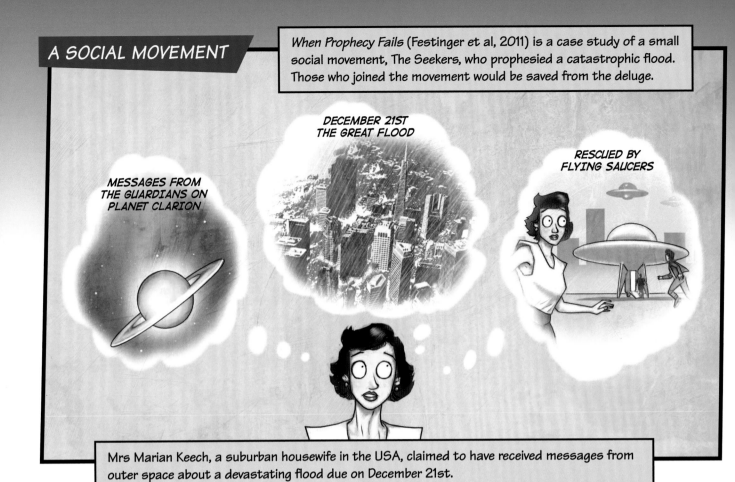

A SOCIAL MOVEMENT

When Prophecy Fails (Festinger et al, 2011) is a case study of a small social movement, The Seekers, who prophesied a catastrophic flood. Those who joined the movement would be saved from the deluge.

Mrs Marian Keech, a suburban housewife in the USA, claimed to have received messages from outer space about a devastating flood due on December 21st.

Case studies show that no two social situations are the same. However, they sometimes show that similar situations produce similar results – as in this case, when prophecy fails people often cling to their beliefs.

LONGITUDINAL STUDIES

Longitudinal studies are designed to study development and change. They examine the same group of people over fairly long periods of time.

The National Child Development Study began with over 17,400 babies born in Britain in March 1958. Here are some of its findings on social inequality.

UPPER CLASS

1958 FATHER – LAWYER

1979 SON – UNIVERSITY DEGREE

1990 WELL-PAID JOB

2000 OWN HOUSE

2004 TRANSPORT

> The class you are born into can have a powerful effect on your life. In general, the higher your class of birth the more likely you are to live a long and healthy life, to have a high income and a high living standard (Elliott and Vaitilingam, 2008).

LOWER CLASS

1958 FATHER – LABOURER

1979 SON – NO QUALIFICATIONS

1990 UNEMPLOYED

2000 RENTED FLAT

2004 TRANSPORT

Starting with a sample of 1,125 young people aged 14 in Merseyside and Greater Manchester, the North West Longitudinal Study tracked them for one or more years from 1991 to 1995. Each year they were given a questionnaire about their attitudes to and use of drugs. The findings were very different from the picture presented by parts of the media and many politicians (Parker et al, 1998).

Tabloid press.

House of Commons.

There was little evidence of pressure from friends to take drugs.

Most drug users were fairly conventional with no criminal record.

By age 18, 59% had tried cannabis, 20% ecstasy, 10% heroin, 6% cocaine.

Many young people saw the occasional and sometimes regular use of 'soft' drugs as a normal part of their recreation.

OFFICIAL STATISTICS

Official statistics are numerical data produced by national and local government bodies. They can be compiled and used in various ways. This unit shows that official statistics should be regarded with considerable caution.

CRIME STATISTICS

The annual Crime Survey for England and Wales asks people if they have been victims of various crimes. The results show a steady reduction in crime from 19 million offences in 1995 to 6.5 million for the year ending in June 2015 (Office for National Statistics, 2015).

CYBERCRIME

Has crime fallen or simply changed? A large-scale survey estimated that in England and Wales there were 5.1 million incidents of fraud in 2014/15, much of it committed online. Questions about online crime or cybercrime have been largely absent from past crime surveys. (Office for National Statistics, 2015).

POLICE STATISTICS

Police crime statistics for England and Wales are based on crimes recorded by the police. They indicate a steady drop in the crime rate from 2003/04 to 2013/14. A study of police crime recording showed that nearly one fifth of crimes reported to the police were not recorded (HMIC, 2014). Improvements in recording may have led to a 3% rise in police recorded crime in 2014/15 (Office for National Statistics, 2015).

Official police crime statistics are based on crimes recorded by the police. They can be affected by the priorities of different police forces.

NON-REPORTING

Many crimes, especially frauds, are not reported the authorities. In the USA in 2011 there were just over one million reports of financial fraud. But, one survey estimated that the actual number was nearly 38 million. The most common reasons for non-reporting are shown in the above picture (Deevy and Beals, 2013).

CORPORATE CRIME

Corporate crimes are crimes committed for the benefit of business corporations. They are difficult to detect and there are no reliable statistics on their extent.

POLITICS AND STATISTICS

Conservative governments changed the method for counting unemployment over 30 times between 1982 and 1992. In nearly every case this led to a drop in the official unemployment figures (Denscombe, 1994).

A change in the methods of police recording resulted in a rise in the official rate of violent crime (UK Statistics Authority, 2010).

STOP AND SEARCH STATISTICS

Reading the Riots is a study based on in-depth interviews with 270 people who took part in the August 2011 riots in England (Guardian, 2011). It found that hostility towards the police was a major reason for the riots. Official statistics on stop and search help to explain this hostility.

STOP AND SEARCH

In England and Wales in 2009/10 black people were seven times more likely to be stopped and searched by the police than white people (Ministry of Justice, 2011). In *Reading the Riots*, 73% of interviewees said they had been stopped and searched in the last year, 71% said more than once (50% of the interviewees were black).

REVENGE

Many saw the riots as revenge for the way police conducted stop and search – for the humiliation, unjust suspicion and discrimination they experienced. (Speech bubbles taken from *Reading the Riots*.)

DOCUMENTS

Documents refer to a wide range of written and recorded material. John Scott (1990) suggests four ways of assessing documents – authenticity, credibility, representativeness and meaning.

AUTHENTICITY

Is the document genuine?

In 1983, the German magazine *Stern* announced that it had acquired Hitler's diaries – 62 handwritten volumes for which it paid $4 million. Research later showed that the diaries were forgeries.

CREDIBILITY

Does the document provide a true picture or does it distort events?

THIS WILL SET THE RECORD STRAIGHT.

Former US president George W. Bush was strongly criticised for authorising 'waterboarding' – a form of torture – for al Qaeda suspects. He claimed in his memoirs that this saved lives. According to British officials, there is no evidence to support this claim.

REPRESENTATIVENESS

Is the document typical or a one-off?

Newspaper headlines

1898 **The avalanche of brutality under the name of Hooliganism** (*Daily Graphic*)

1931 **Street gangs – this greatest menace of the century** (*Reynolds News*)

1955 **War on Teddy Boys – menace in the streets of Britain** (*Daily Dispatch*)

2005 **Yobs are intimidating entire neighbourhoods** (*Daily Mail*)

From the 1800s to the present day, reports in tabloid newspapers have often pictured young men as 'ruffians', 'hooligans' and 'yobs' (Pearson, 1983).

An image of Teddy Boys based on newspaper reports from the 1950s.

What does the document mean to those who produced it, to the people who see or hear it and to the researcher who interprets it?

DISPUTES OVER THE OCCUPIED TERRITORIES CONTINUE.

NEWS...BREAKING NEWS...BREAK

WHAT ARE THE OCCUPIED TERRITORIES?

HAVEN'T A CLUE.

Based on a sample of 300 young people aged 17-22, 71% had no idea what 'occupied territories' meant, 11% thought it was Palestinians occupying Israeli land and only 9% got it right – Israelis occupying Palestinian land (Philo and Miller, 2002).

THIS IS PALESTINIAN LAND. THE UNITED NATIONS SAYS THAT THESE SETTLEMENTS ARE ILLEGAL.

THIS IS NOT OCCUPIED TERRITORY. THIS WAS JEWISH LAND IN BIBLICAL TIMES. IT IS PART OF OUR HOMELAND.

An Israeli settlement on the West Bank, part of the territory occupied by Israel after the Six-Day War in 1967. Comments based on videos shown on YouTube.

'I check cheddar like a food inspector' (from *Public Service Announcement*).

'check' means to collect, 'cheddar' means money.

'I'm out here slingin' (from *Coming of Age*)

'slingin' means selling drugs.

'Can't blow too hard, life's a deck of cards' (from *Fallin'*).

'Can't blow too hard' means 'you can't show off too much or your whole life can tumble'.

Jay-Z translates lines from his songs – taken from his book *Decoded* (2010).

EXCHANGING NOTES

Valerie Hey (1997) studied girls' friendship patterns in two London comprehensive schools. Part of her data came from notes the girls exchanged during their lessons.

15 notes were exchanged between 3 girls in a history lesson. 90% of what they wrote concerned their relations with each other.

One teacher retrieved discarded notes from her waste basket. Other notes were picked up by Valerie Hey who scrabbled around the floor after lessons.

Valerie Hey was concerned about the ethics of collecting private and personal notes without permission.

VISUAL METHODOLOGIES

Visual methodologies are methods used for analysing and interpreting visual images and the meanings people give to them. Visual images include photographs, paintings, posters, cartoons, flags, video games, TV programmes, films and advertisements.

CONTENT ANALYSIS

Content analysis is a method used to analyse words and images. At its simplest, it counts how often particular words, phrases or images occur.

Main characters in video games by gender, race and age

	Males	White people	Adults
In video games	90%	80%	87%
In US population	51%	75%	59%

A large-scale content analysis of characters in video games showed that males, white people and adults were over-represented in comparison to the United States' population, while females, black people, Hispanics and Native Americans were under-represented (D. Williams et al, 2009).

DISCOURSE ANALYSIS

A discourse is a way of knowing, thinking about and acting towards something. Discourse analysis is a way of identifying and analysing discourses. The following examples illustrate a Victorian discourse on prostitutes.

Customers in a brothel and a murdered prostitute. In Victorian times prostitutes were portrayed as 'fallen women' who enjoyed sex, alcohol and the 'low life', dressed provocatively and tended to meet an early death as a result of suicide or murder. The message was 'the wages of sin are death' (Nead, 1988; Rose, 2012).

IDEOLOGY

One way of interpreting images is to see them as ideology – as a means of justifying inequality, as supporting the rich and powerful, as disguising exploitation and keeping the mass of the population in their place.

Hugh Capet anointed with holy oil as King of France in 987. He now ruled by divine right – by the 'Grace of God'.

A billboard sponsored by the National Association of Manufacturers during the Great Depression. In the foreground are African-American refugees from low-income areas of Louisville after the flood of 1937.

IMAGES IN SOCIETY

Societies are made up of different social groups – for example, regional, ethnic and class groups. To some extent, each group will give their own meaning to images which will be influenced by their position in society.

In 2015, a young white supremacist shot and killed 9 African Americans in a church in Charleston, South Carolina. He was photographed with a Confederate flag, a flag which since the Civil War was a symbol of the Confederacy which fought, in part, to preserve slavery. After the shooting, the state legislature voted to remove the flag from outside the statehouse.

SOCIAL FACTS

Social facts are aspects of society which direct people's behaviour. They can be social relationships like marriage or social institutions like religion.

DURKHEIM AND SUICIDE

Emile Durkheim looked at two social facts – the level of social integration and the rate of suicide. He argued that the greater the level of social integration the lower the level of suicide. In highly integrated groups control over behaviour is strong and there will be considerable pressure against suicide.

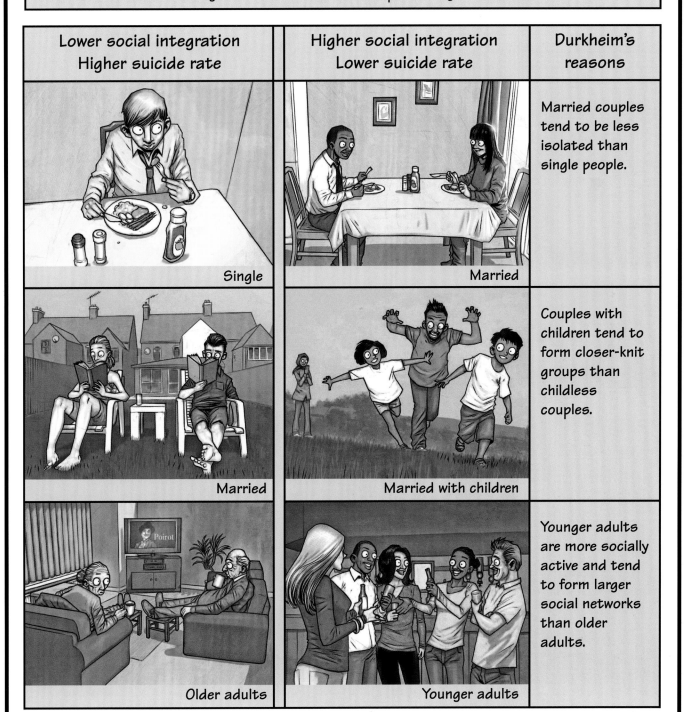

Lower social integration Higher suicide rate	Higher social integration Lower suicide rate	Durkheim's reasons
Single	Married	Married couples tend to be less isolated than single people.
Married	Married with children	Couples with children tend to form closer-knit groups than childless couples.
Older adults	Younger adults	Younger adults are more socially active and tend to form larger social networks than older adults.

Lower social integration Higher suicide rate	Higher social integration Lower suicide rate	Durkheim's reasons
 City dwellers	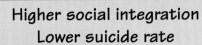 Country dwellers	Village communities are likely to be more integrated than urban areas.
 Protestants	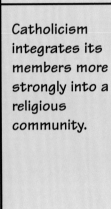 Catholics	Catholicism integrates its members more strongly into a religious community.
 Peace	 War	By identifying a common enemy, war is more likely to unify a nation than peace.

SOCIAL CONSTRUCTION

The idea of social construction provides an alternative to social facts. It argues that people construct meanings which form social reality. The job of the sociologist is to discover these meanings. So, when studying suicide, sociologists should discover the meanings used to categorise deaths as suicide.

In *Discovering Suicide*, J. Maxwell Atkinson (1978) argues that coroners have a 'commonsense theory of suicide' which includes a 'typical suicide biography' and a 'typical suicide death'. The nearer a death fits this theory, the more likely it will be defined as suicide.

POSITIVISM AND INTERPRETIVISM

Some sociologists identify two main approaches to research – positivism and interpretivism. Others reject this distinction, saying there are many different approaches.

Positivism focuses on social facts, on quantitative data and cause and effect relationships.

I'VE BEEN CALLED A POSITIVIST BECAUSE I LIKE TO MEASURE THINGS AND I LIKE MY DATA IN NUMBERS.

I LIKE QUESTIONNAIRES AND SOCIAL SURVEYS BASED ON REPRESENTATIVE SAMPLES.

I WANT TO FIND CORRELATIONS BETWEEN SOCIAL FACTS WHICH INDICATE CAUSAL RELATIONSHIPS.

INTERPRETIVISM

Interpretivism focuses on interpreting the meanings which are seen to direct human action. It favours qualitative data.

Coroner's Court

WHAT ARE THE MEANINGS HE USES TO DEFINE SUICIDE?

CAN YOU DESCRIBE A TYPICAL SUICIDE DEATH?

DROWNING, DRUG OVERDOSE, HANGING, GASSING.

DO I HAVE TO CHOOSE?

J.Maxwell Atkinson used observation and in-depth interviews in his research on suicide.

Many sociologists use a variety of research methods and both quantitative and qualitative data.

REFLEXIVITY

Sociologists are increasingly concerned with *reflexivity*. This means reflecting on yourself and your research. How have I as a person and the way I conducted my research affected the data which I produced?

BILL WHYTE

Know yourself (Whyte, 1993). See page 8.

Reflect on your research. 'During my research I learned when to ask questions and when not to, as well as what questions to ask' (Whyte, 1955).

LOOKING BACK

This was part of an interview with Jay Butler, an African-American disc jockey at WCHB Radio in Detroit.

During the late 1960s and 70s, many African Americans rejected the idea that 'white is right' and replaced it with 'I'm black and I'm proud'. The researcher argued that this view was reflected in soul music. He later wondered whether he'd asked a leading question in order to support his argument (Haralambos, 1994).

In her study of prostitution, Julia O'Connell Davidson participated as one of the receptionists in Desiree's brothel. She found that 'my identity as a woman affected the data I collected'. Both clients and workers were more likely to talk freely and feel at ease with a woman rather than a man (O'Connell Davidson and Layder, 1994).

ACCEPTANCE

As part of her research on the police, Meghan Hollis went to observe a fight on a Saturday night outside a club in a New England city.

Despite her discomfort, Meghan spent a further 4 hours on patrol with the officer. She had proved herself in a male-dominated occupation. As a result she gained the trust, respect and cooperation of the police (Hollis, 2014).

CONSTRUCTING DATA

Most sociologists argue that to some extent research data are constructions based on interpretations made by researchers. Some of the factors which might influence these interpretations are outlined below.

MULTIPLE CONSTRUCTIONS

Some sociologists have argued that if data are constructed from interpretations, then there is no 'objective reality' outside those interpretations. All we are left with is a multitude of constructions, none right and none wrong.

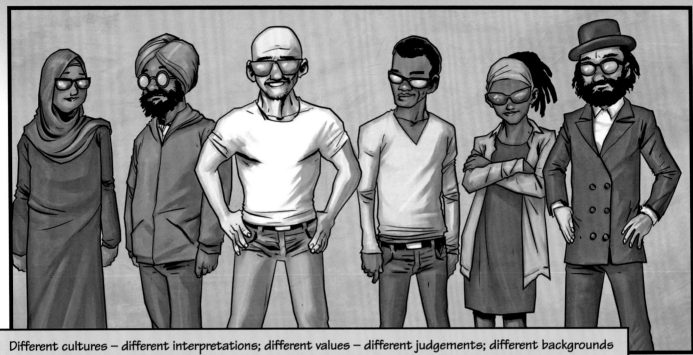

Different cultures – different interpretations; different values – different judgements; different backgrounds – different perspectives. Does this mean there is no reality apart from these multiple constructions?

All sociologists agree that human beings interpret the world. But this does not mean that there is no reality separate from their interpretations, that there is 'no solid world out there separate from their concepts and beliefs' (O'Connell Davidson and Layder, 1994).

REALITY AND INTERPRETATION

Legend states that King Canute, who ruled England from 1016 to 1035, believed that he had the power to turn back the incoming tide. Tested against reality, this belief was found to be sadly wanting.

A TREE THAT FALLS IN THE FOREST, FALLS REGARDLESS OF WHETHER A PERSON IS THERE TO WITNESS AND INTERPRET THE EVENT.

Julia O'Connell Davidson (O'Connell Davidson and Layder, 1994)

BETTER RESEARCH

Today, sociologists accept that complete objectivity is impossible. They recognise that, to some extent, researchers must construct data. But this does not mean giving up on the pursuit of better research, and more objective investigations.

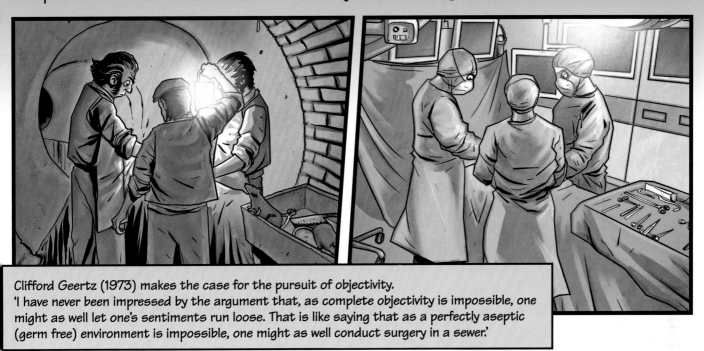

Clifford Geertz (1973) makes the case for the pursuit of objectivity.
'I have never been impressed by the argument that, as complete objectivity is impossible, one might as well let one's sentiments run loose. That is like saying that as a perfectly aseptic (germ free) environment is impossible, one might as well conduct surgery in a sewer.'

IMPROVING RESEARCH

One way of improving research is to be aware of possible problems. Here the authors of two classic participation observation studies outlined earlier, look back on their research (see pages 8 and 9).

'They saw first of all a white man and this was a barrier between us. But the disadvantage of being white was offset in part by the fact that, as an outsider, I was not a competitor' (Liebow, 1967).

At first Bill Whyte tried to fit in by trying to act like the Italian-American gang he was observing. 'I soon learned that people did not expect me to be just like them' (Whyte, 1993).

VALUES AND RESEARCH

Sociology used to be known as the 'science of society'. Many sociologists believed that an objective, value-free study of society was possible. Today, many sociologists see the whole research process, from the choice of topic to the interpretation of the data, as influenced by researchers' values.

WHOSE SIDE ARE WE ON?

The American sociologist Howard Becker (1970) argues that it is impossible to conduct research 'uncontaminated by personal and political sympathies'. His sympathies are with the 'underdog' – the poor and the powerless.

ALVIN GOULDNER

Like Becker, Alvin Goulder (1971, 1975) believes that a value-free sociology is impossible. His political views lead him to condemn the system of social inequality which generates poverty and powerlessness.

VALUES AND THEORY

Gouldner argues that values underlie all sociological theories. And theories influence research directing what to look for and how to interpret it. Marxist theory provides an example.

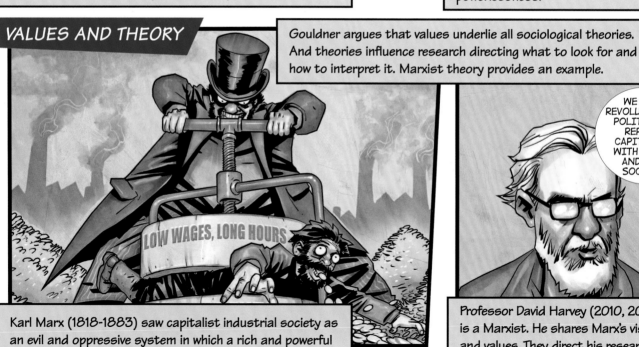

Karl Marx (1818-1883) saw capitalist industrial society as an evil and oppressive system in which a rich and powerful ruling class own the factories and exploit the workers.

Professor David Harvey (2010, 2014) is a Marxist. He shares Marx's vision and values. They direct his research and the questions he asks.

STANDPOINT THEORY

Standpoint theory conducts research from the standpoint of a particular group. These groups are often oppressed and experience discrimination – for example, women, ethnic minorities and people with disabilities. Standpoint theorists reject the view that researchers should necessarily guard against their background as a source of error and distortion. They argue that the researcher's position in society – for example as a woman – may give them a unique vantage point and valuable insights and special knowledge (Hammersley, 2011).

BEING A WOMAN

Glass ceiling

Domestic violence

Researcher

I KNOW WHAT QUESTIONS TO ASK.

According to standpoint theory, a female researcher, because of her experience as a woman, is more likely to obtain a deeper understanding of women than a male researcher.

DIFFERENCES

Critics of standpoint theory argue that it has been developed largely by white middle-class women and tends to ignore the many differences in background and experience between women (Alvesson and Sköldberg, 2009)

I'M BLACK. WHAT DO YOU KNOW ABOUT RACISM?

I'M A LESBIAN. YOU DON'T KNOW WHAT IT'S LIKE TO EXPERIENCE HOMOPHOBIA.

I'M WORKING CLASS. WHAT DO YOU KNOW ABOUT MY CLASS POSITION?

RESEARCH ETHICS

Research ethics are the moral guidelines for researchers. Participants must be informed about the research, they must not be deceived, their consent must be given, they have the right to withdraw, they must be protected from discomfort and harm, their privacy should not be invaded and their identity kept secret.

MILGRAM'S OBEDIENCE EXPERIMENT

The American psychologist Stanley Milgram (1963) conducted an experiment to see how far people would obey commands which they felt were wrong and would harm others. The participants were told that the experiment was a 'scientific study' of the effect of punishment – electric shocks – on learning. Unknown to the participants, the shocks were not real.

The man on the right is an actor. He is pretending to suffer extreme pain. The man in the middle is also an actor.

Milgram justifies his research methods: 'This experiment is important. If one man in a white coat can get people to harm others, think what governments can command.'

THE 'TEAROOM TRADE'

Laud Humphreys (1970) studied casual sex between men in public toilets in the USA. This is known as the 'tearoom trade' in gay slang.

Humphreys acted as a 'watchqueen' warning of the approach of strangers and the police. He kept his identity as a researcher secret.

I'M FROM THE HEALTH SERVICE. THANKS FOR AGREEING TO THIS INTERVIEW.

A year later, Humphreys interviewed some of the men he had observed. The interviews were conducted in their homes. Humphreys changed his appearance and pretended that he was doing a survey on health. He tracked down their names and addresses from their licence plate numbers.

I HAD TO KEEP MY RESEARCH SECRET AND INVADE THE MEN'S PRIVACY IN ORDER TO CONDUCT THE STUDY.

Humphreys defends his methods. His research showed that the participants were not 'dangerous deviants' – most were 'respectable' married men.

Alvesson, M. & Skölderberg, K (2009). *Reflexive methodology: New vistas for qualitative research,* (2nd ed.). London: Sage.

ASH (Action on Smoking and Health) (2016). *Smoking statistics.* www.ash.org.uk

Atkinson, J.M. (1978). *Discovering suicide.* London: Macmillan.

Becker, H.S. (1970). *Sociological work.* New Brunswick: Transaction Books.

Becker, H.S. (1971). Social-class variations in the teacher-pupil relationship. In B.R.Cosin et al (eds.), *School and society.* London: Routledge.

Belot, M. & James, J. (2009). *Healthy school meals and educational outcomes.* Colchester: Institute for Social and Economic Research.

Bloor, M. (1997). *Selected writings in medical sociological research.* Aldershot: Ashgate.

Boellstorff, T. (2006). A ludicrous discipline? Ethnography and game studies. *Games and Culture,* 1, 29-35.

Boellstorff, T., Nardi, B., Pearce, C. & Taylor, T.L. (2012). *Ethnography and virtual worlds: A handbook of method.* Princeton: Princeton University Press.

Brawn, V. & Clarke, V. (2013). *Successful qualitative research: A practical guide for beginners.* London: Sage.

Bruce, S. (1995). Religion and the sociology of religion. In M.Haralambos (ed.), *Developments in Sociology, Volume 11.* Ormskirk: Causeway Press.

Bryman, A. (2008). *Social research methods* (3rd edition). Oxford: Oxford University Press.

Chaundhary, V. & Walker, M. (1996). The petty crime war. *The Guardian,* 21.11.1996.

Cicourel, A.V. (1976). *The social organisation of juvenile justice.* London: Heinemann.

Cumberbatch, G. (1994). Legislating mythology: Video violence and children. *Journal of Mental Health,* 3, 485-494.

Deevy, M. & Beals, M. (2013). *The scope of the problem: An overview of fraud prevalence measurement.* Stanford, CA: Financial Fraud Research Center.

Denscombe, M. (1994). *Sociology update.* Leicester: Olympus Books.

Ditton, J. (1977). *Part-time crime: An ethnography of fiddling and pilferage.* London: Macmillan.

Durkheim, E. (1970, originally 1897). *Suicide: A study in sociology.* London: Routledge & Kegan Paul.

Elliot, J. & Vaitilingam, R. (eds.) (2008). *Now we are 50: Key findings from the National Child Development Study, summary report.* London: Institute of Education, University of London.

ESDS (Economic and Social Data Service). (2011). *Guide to the National Child Development Study.*

Festinger, L., Riecken, H.W. & Schachter, S. (2011 edition). *When prophecy fails.* Blacksburg, VA: Wilder Publications.

Flanders, N. (1970). *Analysing teacher behaviour.* Reading, MA: Addison-Wesley.

Fitzpatrick, A. & Grant, C. (2011). *The 2010/11 British Crime Survey: Technical report, Volume 1.* London: Home Office.

Geertz, C. (1973). *The interpretation of cultures.* New York: Basic Books.

Global Drug Survey: 2014 findings (2014). http://www.globaldrugsurvey.com/custom-surveys/methodology/

Global Drug Survey: Methodology (2014). http://www.globaldrugsurvey.com/custom-surveys/methodology/

Gouldner, A.W. (1971). *The coming crisis of Western sociology.* London: Heinemann.

Grogan, S. & Richards, H. (2002). Body image: Focus groups with boys and men. *Men and Masculinities,* 4, 219-232.

Guardian. (2011). *Reading the riots.* Various issue of *The Guardian* 05.12.2011–10.12.2011.

Hadaway, C.K., Marler, P.L. & Chaves, M. (1993). What polls don't show: A closer look at US church attendance. *American Sociological Review,* vol. 58.

Hammersley, M. (2011). *Methodology: Who needs it?* London: Sage.

Haralambos, M. (1994). *Right on: From blues to soul in black America.* Ormskirk: Causeway Press.

Hargreaves, D.H. (1967). *Social relations in a secondary school.* London: Routledge & Kegan Paul.

Harvey, D. (2010). *The enigma of capital and the crises of capitalism.* London: Profile Books.

Harvey, D. (2014). *Seventeen contradictions and the end of capitalism.* London: Profile Books.

Heelas, P. & Woodhead, L. (2005). *The spiritual revolution: Why religion is giving way to spirituality.* Oxford: Blackwell.

HESA (Higher Education Statistics Agency) (2016). *Students in higher education.* www.hesa.ac.uk

Hey, V. (1997). *The company she keeps: An ethnography of girls' friendships.* Buckingham: Open University Press.

HMIC (2014). *Crime-recording: Making the victim count.* London, HMIC.

Hollis, M.E. (2014). Accessing the experiences of female and minority police officers: Observations from an ethnographic researcher. In K. Lumsden and A. Winter (eds.), *Reflexivity in criminological research: Experiences with the powerful and the powerless.* Houndmills : Palgrave Macmillan.

Humphreys, L. (1970). *Tearoom trade: Impersonal sex in public places.* London: Duckworth.

Jay-Z. (2010). *Decoded.* London: Virgin Books.

REFERENCES

Johnson, T.P. et al (2002). *A validation of the Crowne-Marlowe social desirability scale.* Chicago: Survey Research Laboratory, University of Illinois at Chicago.

Klineberg, O. (1971). Race and IQ. *Courier*, 24, 10.

Labov, W. (1973). The logic of non-standard English. In N. Keddie (ed.), *Tinker, tailor...the myth of cultural deprivation.* Harmondsworth: Penguin.

LaPiere, R.T. (1934). Attitudes vs. actions. *Social Forces*, 13, 230-237.

Lewis, O. (1951). *Life in a Mexican village: Tepoztlan restudied.* Urbana IL: University of Illinois Press.

Liebow, E. (1967). *Tally's corner.* Boston, MA: Little, Brown.

Loftus, E.F. (2003). Our changeable memories: Legal and practical applications, *Nature*, 4, 231-234.

Maguire, M. (2000). Researching 'street criminals': A neglected art. In R.D.King & E.Wincup (eds.), *Doing research on crime and justice.* Oxford: Oxford University Press.

Mair, G. (2000). Research on community penalties. In R.D.King & E.Wincup (eds.), *Doing research on crime and justice.* Oxford: Oxford University Press.

Malinowski, B. (1922). *Argonauts of the Western Pacific.* London: George Routledge & Sons.

Martin, D. (1969). *The religious and the secular.* London: Routledge and Kegan Paul.

McGreal, C. (2011). America's crime rate is plunging, but is it really down to locking up more people? *The Guardian*, 22.08.2011.

Milgram, S. (1974). *Obedience to authority.* London: Tavistock.

Ministry of Justice. (2011). *Statistics on race and the criminal justice system.* London: National Statistics.

National Centre for Social Research (2010). *British social attitudes: The 26th report.* London: Sage.

Nead, L. (1988). *Myths of sexuality: Representations of women in Victorian Britain.* Oxford: Blackwell.

Office for National Statistics (2015). *User guide to crime statistics for England and Wales.* London: Office for National Statistics.

Office for National Statistics (2016). *Marriages in England and Wales.* www.ons.gov.uk

O'Connell Davidson, J. & Layder, D. (1994). *Methods, sex and madness.* London: Routledge.

O'Connor, H. & Madge, C. (2001). Cyber-mothers: Online synchronous interviewing using conferencing software. *Sociological Research Online*, vol.5, no.4.

Parker, H., Aldridge, J. & Measham, F. (1998). *Illegal leisure: The normalisation of adolescent recreational drug use.* London: Routledge.

Parker, M. (2000). *Organisational culture and identity.* London: Sage.

Pearce, C. (2006). *Playing ethnography: A study of emergent behaviour in online games and virtual worlds.* London: SMARTlab Centre.

Pearce, C. (2009). *Communities of play: Emergent cultures in online games and virtual worlds.* Cambridge, MA: MIT Press.

Piff, K.P. et al (2012). Higher social class predicts increased unethical behaviour. *Proceedings of the National Academy of Sciences*, vol. 109, no. 11.

Pearson, G. (1983). *Hooligan: A history of respectable fears.* Basingstoke: Macmillan.

Redfield, R. (1930). *Tepoztlan: A Mexican village.* Chicago: University of Chicago Press.

Rose, G. (2012). *Visual methodologies: An introduction to researching with visual materials* (3rd ed.). London: Sage.

Rosenthal, R. & Jacobson, L. (1968). *Pygmalion in the classroom.* New York: Holt, Rinehart & Winston.

Russell, D. (1986). *The secret trauma: Incest in the lives of girls and women.* New York: Basic Books.

Social Trends. (2011). Basingstoke: Palgrave Macmillan.

Silverman, D. (2010). *Doing qualitative research* (4th ed.). London: Sage.

Silverman, D. (2015). *Interpreting qualitative data* (5th ed.). London: Sage.

Skeggs, B. (1994). Situating the production of feminist ethnography. In M. Maynard & J. Purvis (eds.), *Researching women's lives.* Basingstoke: Taylor and Francis.

Skeggs, B. (1997). Formations of class and gender: Becoming respectable. London: Sage.

Stands In Timber, J. & Liberty, M. (1967). *Cheyenne Memories.* New Haven: Yale University Press.

Taylor, T.L. (2002). Living digitally: Embodiment in virtual worlds. In R. Schroeder (ed.), *The social life of avatars: Presence and interaction in shared virtual environments.* London: Springer-Verlag.

Venkatesh, S. (2009). *Gang leader for a day.* London: Penguin.

Walklate, S. (2000). Researching victims. In R.D.King & Wincup.E. (eds.), *Doing research on crime and justice.* Oxford: Oxford University Press.

Whyte, William F. (1955). *Street corner society* (revised edition). Chicago: University of Chicago Press.

Whyte, William F. (1993). *Street corner society* (4th ed.). Chicago: University of Chicago Press.

Wight, D. (1994). Boys' thoughts and talk about sex in a working-class locality of Glasgow. *Sociological Review*, 42, 702-737.

Williams, D. et al (2009). The virtual census: Representations of gender, race and age in video games. *New Media & Society*, 11, 5, 815-834.

Zimring, F.E. (2007). *The great American crime decline.* New York: Oxford University Press, Inc.